Traditional Hymns

Complements All Piano Methods

Table of Contents

Traditional Hymns Level 5 is designed for use with the fifth book of any piano method.

Concepts in *Level 5:*

Range

Symbols

pp, p, mp, mf, f, ff, sfz, ♯, ♭, ♮, *rit.*, *a tempo*, *sim.*, *8va*, *loco*, D.S. al Fine, 𝄋, D.S. al Coda, 𝄌, ⌢

cresc. ——————— *dim.*

Rhythm

time signatures: $\frac{2}{4}$ $\frac{3}{4}$ $\frac{4}{4}$ ¢ $\frac{3}{8}$ $\frac{6}{8}$

 swing eighths

Scales/Keys

Major: C G F D B♭

Chords

M, m, aug., dim.   1st and 2nd inversions

ISBN 978-0-634-03681-1

HAL•LEONARD® CORPORATION

7777 W. BLUEMOUND RD. P.O. BOX 13819 MILWAUKEE, WI 53213

Visit Hal Leonard Online at
www.halleonard.com

Blessed Assurance

Lyrics by Fanny J. Crosby
Music by Phoebe Palmer Knapp
Arranged by Fred Kern

Rejoice, The Lord Is King

Words by Charles Wesley
Music by John Darwall
Arranged by Mona Rejino

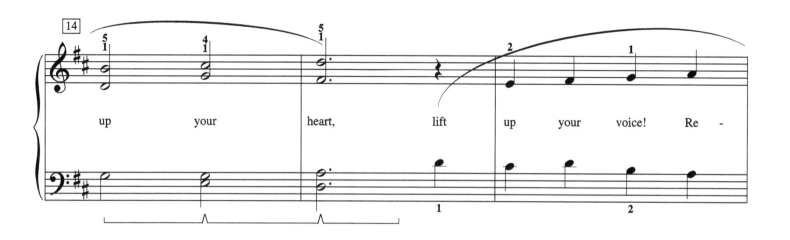

up   your   heart,   lift   up   your   voice!   Re -

joice,   a - gain   I   say,   re -   joice!   His

cresc.   *f*

King - dom   can - not   fail,   He   rules   o'er   earth   and

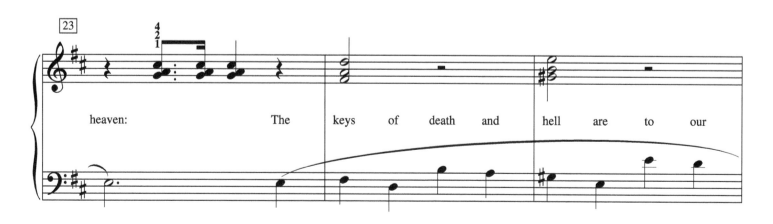

heaven: The   keys   of   death   and   hell   are   to   our

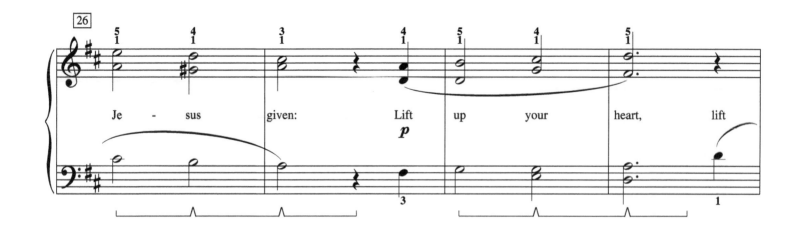

Je - sus given: Lift up your heart, lift

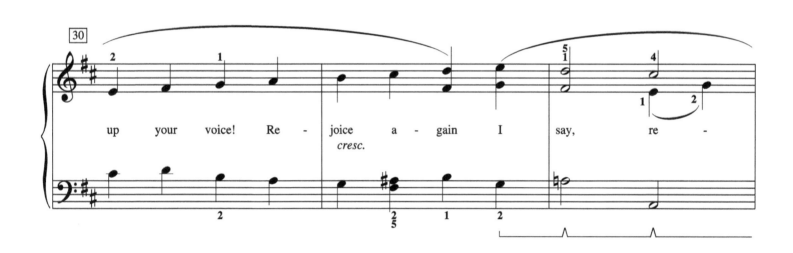

up your voice! Re - joice a - gain I say, re -

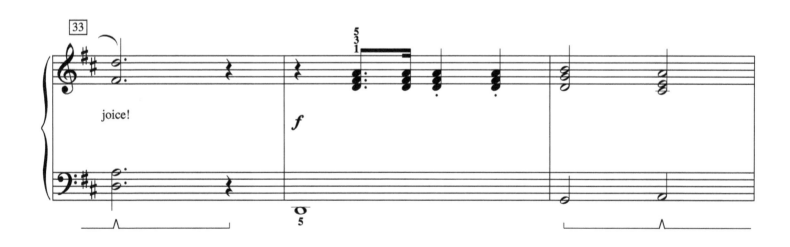

joice!

Open My Eyes, That I May See

Words and Music by
Clara H. Scott
Arranged by Phillip Keveren

will to see; O - pen my eyes, il - lu - mine me, *cresc.*

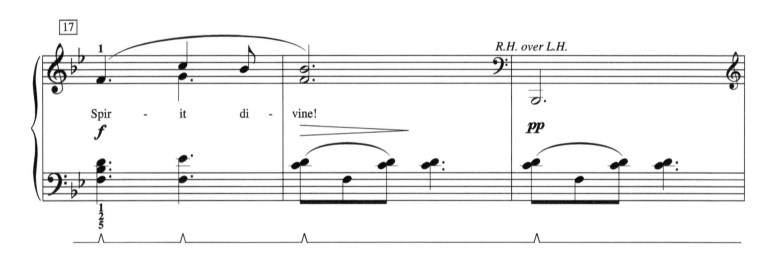

Spir - it di - vine! **f** *R.H. over L.H.* **pp**

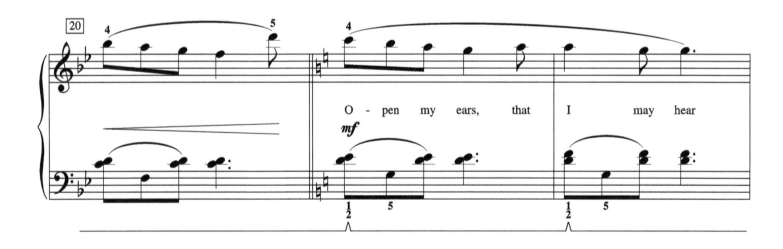

O - pen my ears, that I may hear **mf**

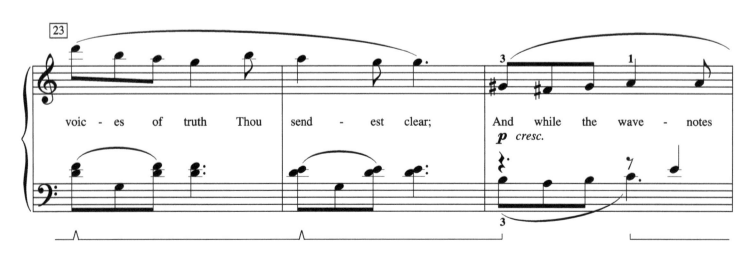

voic - es of truth Thou send - est clear; And while the wave - notes **p** *cresc.*

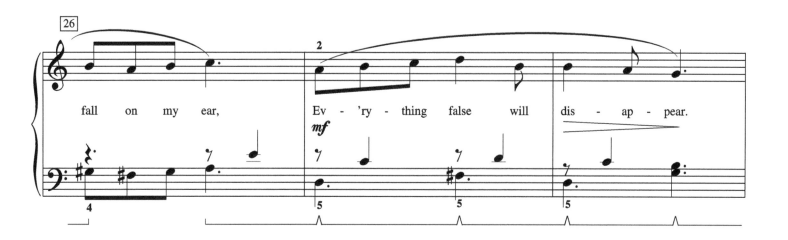

fall on my ear, Ev - 'ry - thing false will dis - ap - pear.

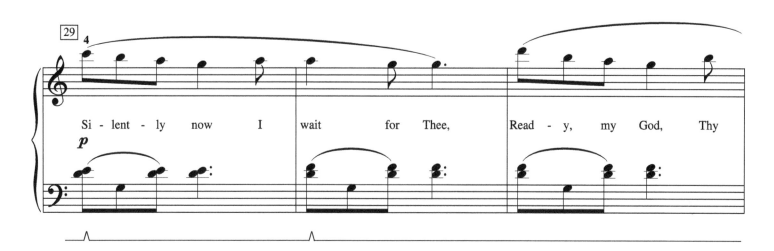

Si - lent - ly now I wait for Thee, Read - y, my God, Thy

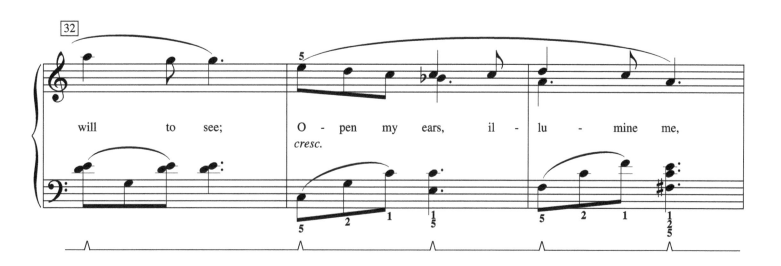

will to see; O - pen my ears, il - lu - mine me,

Spir - it di - vine!

rit. e dim. to end

R.H. over L.H.

9

Swing Low, Sweet Chariot

Traditional Spiritual
Arranged by Mona Rejino

looked   o - ver Jor - dan,   and   what did   I   see, ___   com - ing   for   to   car - ry   me

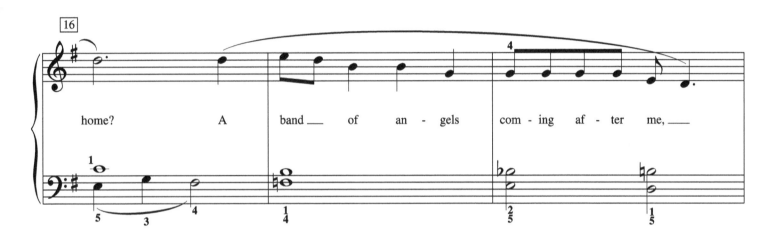

home?   A   band ___   of   an - gels   com - ing   af - ter   me, ___

com - ing   for   to   car - ry   me   home.   Swing

D.S. al Coda

CODA

home.
poco a poco rit.

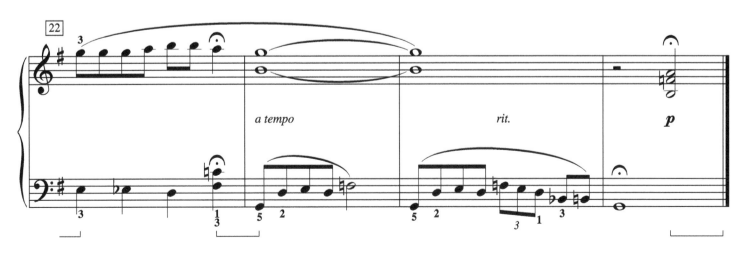

a tempo   *rit.*

Be Thou My Vision

Traditional Irish
Translated by Mary E. Byrne
Arranged by Phillip Keveren

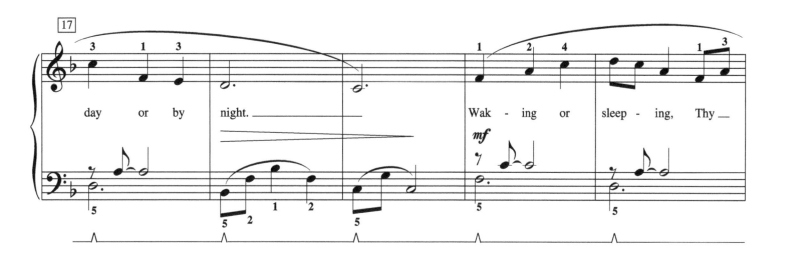

day or by night. _____ Wak - ing or sleep - ing, Thy _____

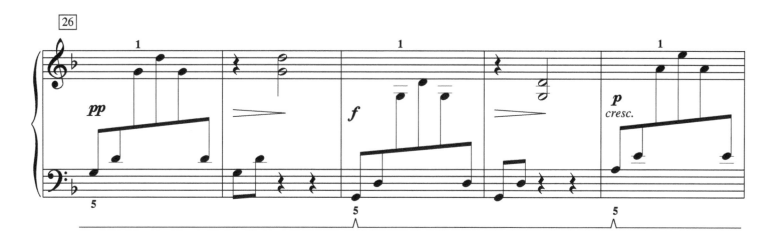

pres - ence my light.

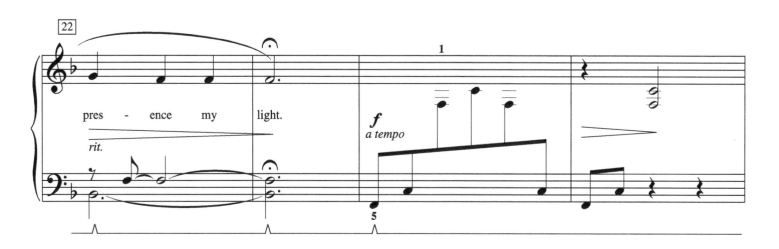

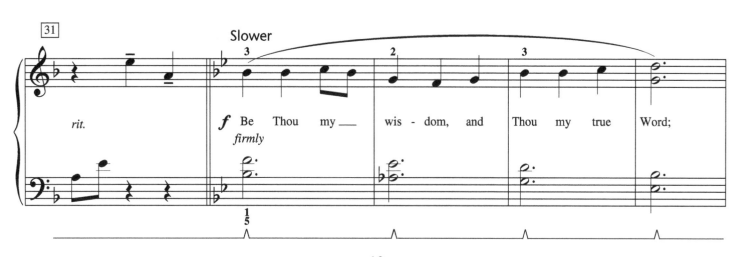

rit. *f* Be Thou my _____ wis - dom, and Thou my true Word;

13

I ev - er with Thee and Thou with me, Lord;

Thou my great Fa - ther, I Thy true son,

Thou in me dwell - ing, and I with Thee one.

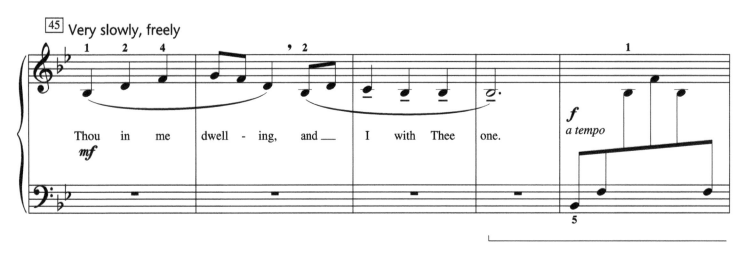

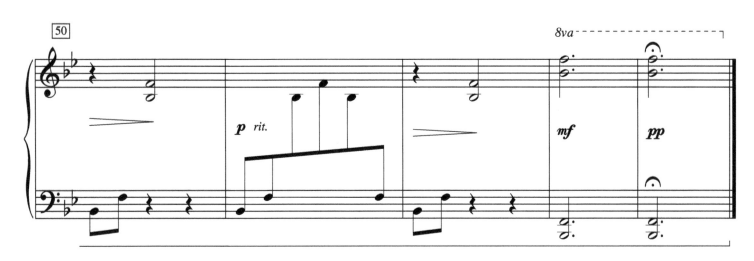

14

Church In The Wildwood

Words and Music by
Dr. William S. Pitts
Arranged by Phillip Keveren

wild - wood, oh, come to the church in the vale. No ___

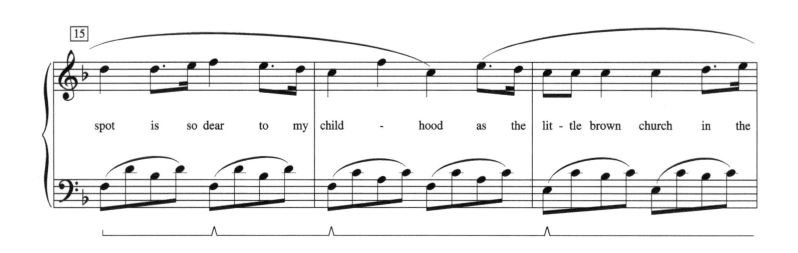

spot is so dear to my child - hood as the lit - tle brown church in the

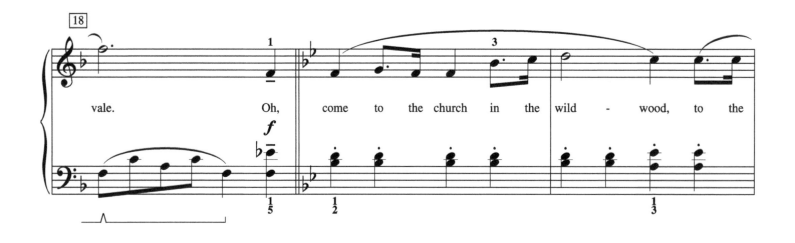

vale. Oh, come to the church in the wild - wood, to the

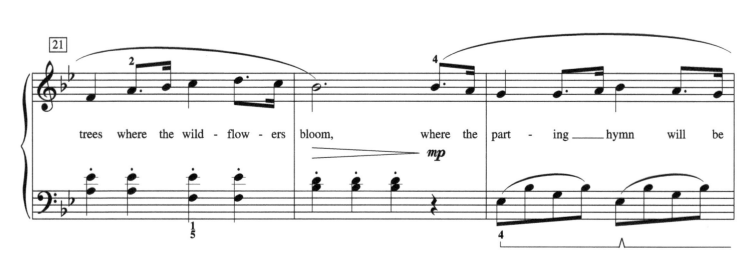

trees where the wild - flow - ers bloom, where the part - ing ___ hymn will be

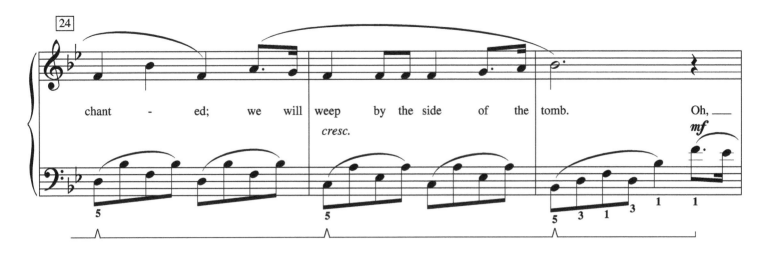

chant - ed; we will weep by the side of the tomb. Oh, ___

come, come, come, come. Come to the church in the wild - wood, oh,

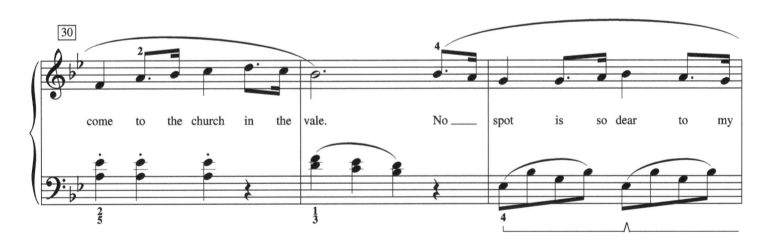

come to the church in the vale. No ___ spot is so dear to my

child - hood as the lit - tle brown church in the vale.

This Little Light Of Mine

African-American Spiritual
Arranged by Fred Kern

With a swing (♩ = 60)

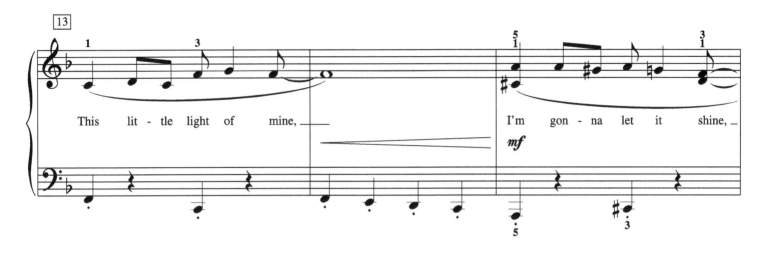

This lit - tle light of mine, ____ I'm gon - na let it shine, ____

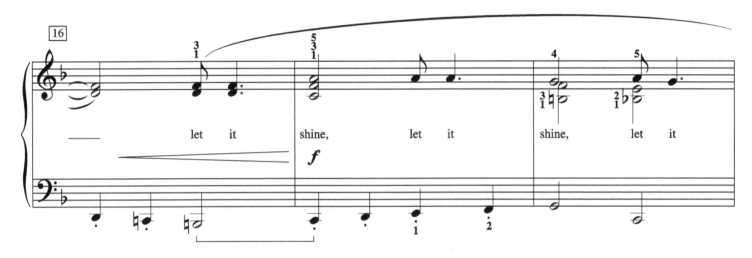

____ let it shine, let it shine, let it

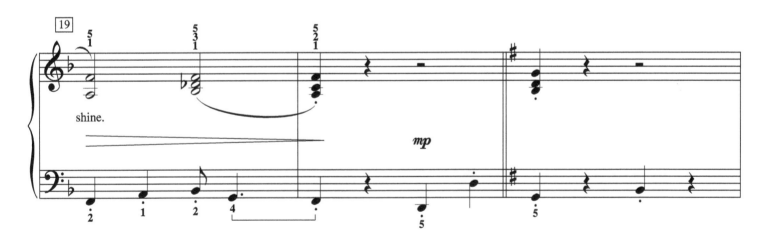

shine.

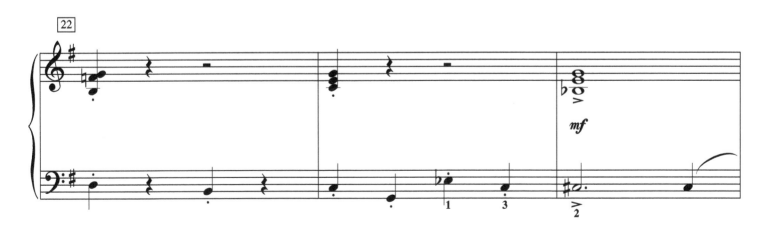

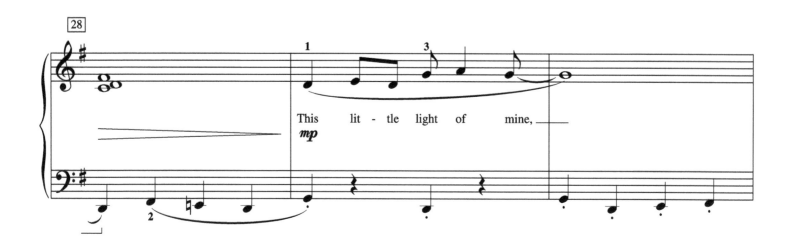

This lit - tle light of mine, ___
mp

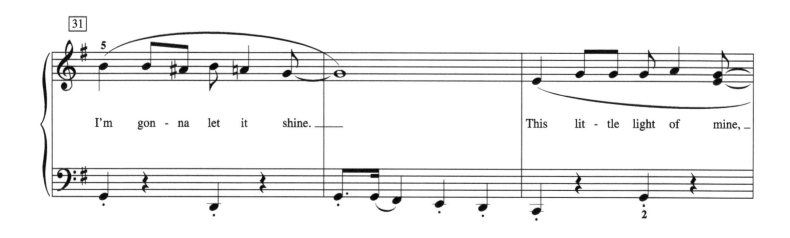

I'm gon - na let it shine. ___ This lit - tle light of mine, ___

I'm gon - na let it shine. ___

I've Got Peace Like A River

Traditional
Arranged by Fred Kern

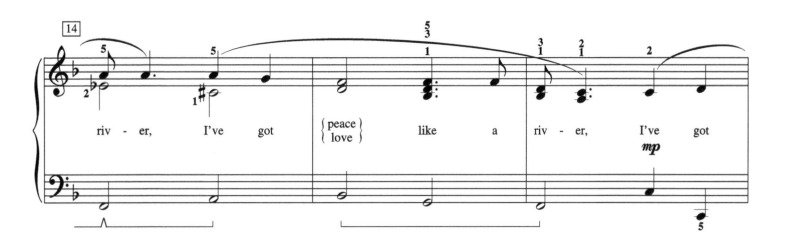

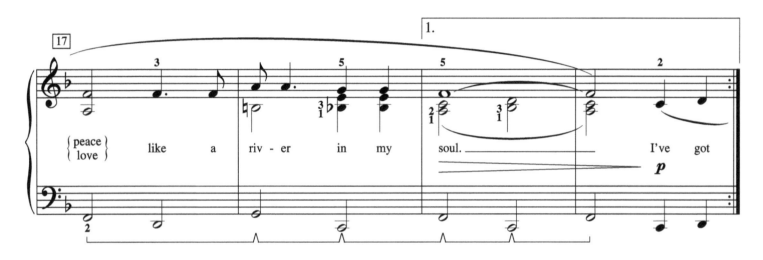

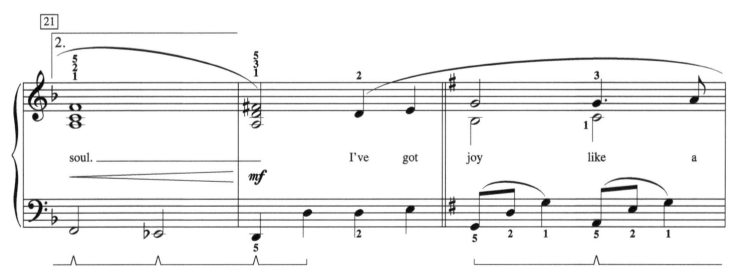

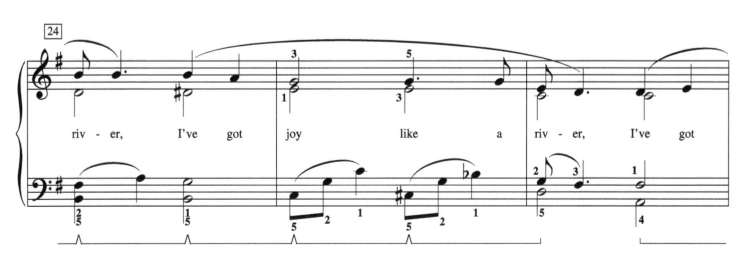

joy   like   a   riv - er   in my   soul; _____
_____ I've   got   joy   like   a   riv - er,   I've   got
joy   like   a   riv - er,   I've   got   joy   like   a
riv - er   in   my   soul. _____

Savior, Like A Shepherd Lead Us

Words from Hymns For The Young
Attributed to Dorothy A. Thrupp
Music by William B. Bradbury
Arranged by Phillip Keveren

pare. Bless-ed Je - sus, Bless-ed Je - sus, Thou hast bought us, Thine we
mp

are; Bless - ed Je - sus, Bless-ed Je - sus, Thou hast bought us, Thine we
mf *rit.* *mp*

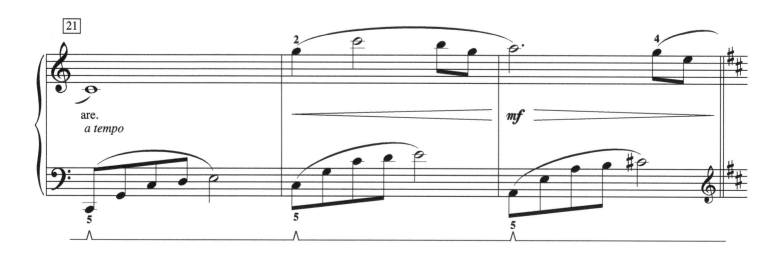

are. We are Thine; do Thou be - friend
a tempo

We are Thine; do Thou be - friend us, Be the Guard-ian of our
p

26

way; Keep Thy flock, from sin de - fend _____ us, _____

Seek us when we go a - stray. Bless - ed Je - sus, bless - ed

Je - sus, Hear, O hear us when we pray; Bless - ed Je - sus, bless - ed

Je - sus, Hear, O hear us when we pray.

Jesus Loves Even Me

(I Am So Glad)

Words and Music by
Philip P. Bliss
Arranged by Mona Rejino

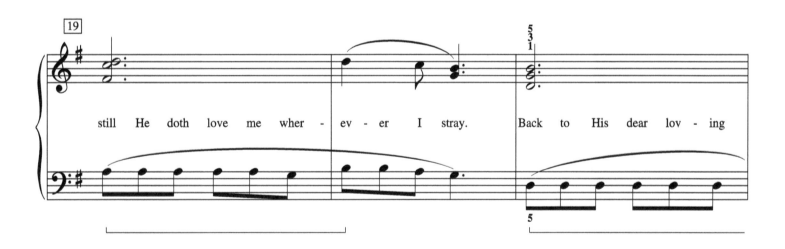

In The Garden

Words and Music by
C. Austin Miles
Arranged by Phillip Keveren

talks with me, and He tells me I am His own; _____ and the

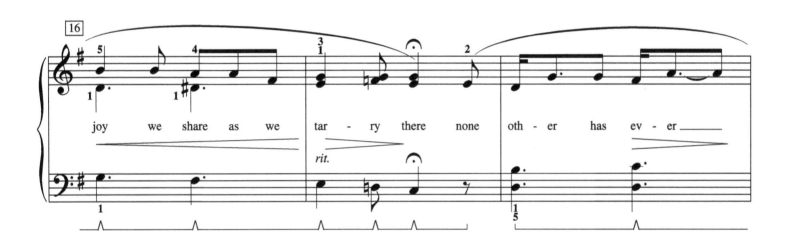

joy we share as we tar - ry there none oth - er has ev - er _____

rit.

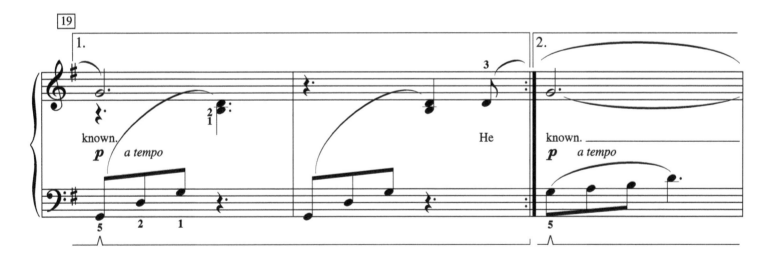

1.

known.

p *a tempo*

He

2.

known. _____

p *a tempo*

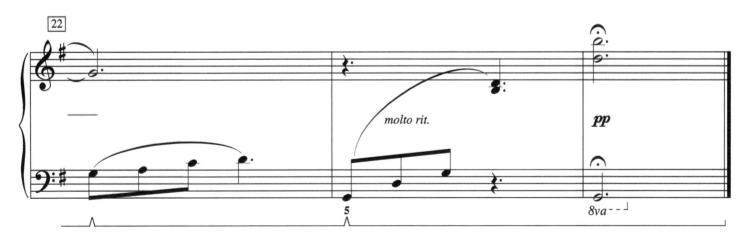

molto rit.

pp

8va - -

Sweet Hour Of Prayer

Words by William W. Walford
Music by William B. Bradbury
Arranged by Fred Kern

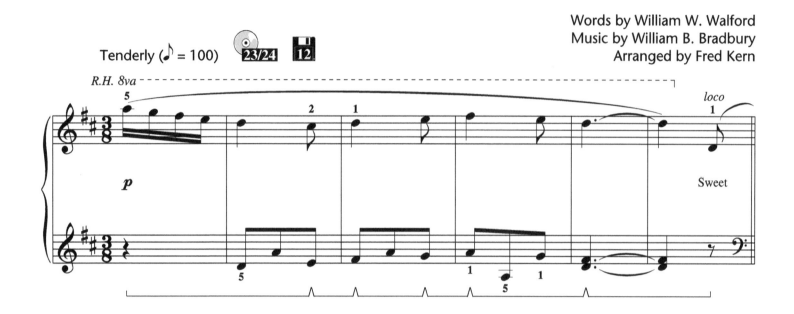

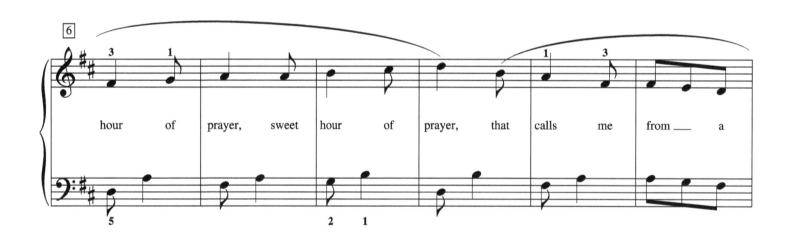

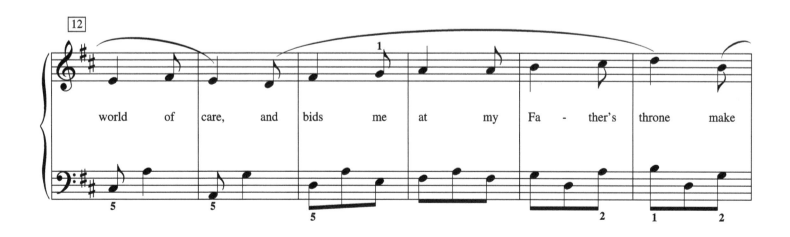

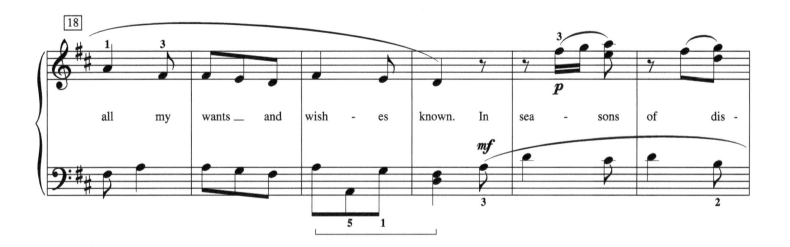

all my wants __ and wish - es known. In sea - sons of dis -

tress and grief, my soul has of - ten found re - lief, and

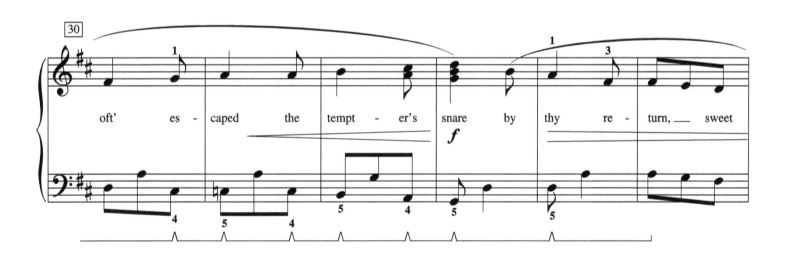

oft' es - caped the tempt - er's snare by thy re - turn, __ sweet

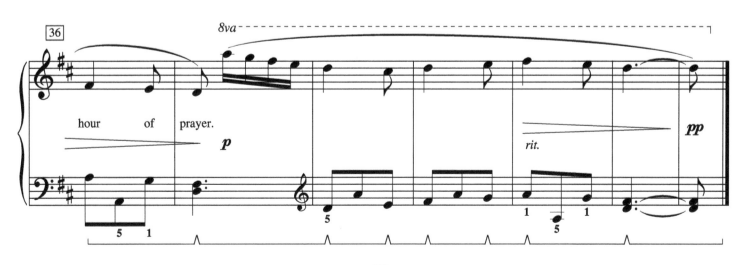

hour of prayer.

Give Me Oil In My Lamp

Traditional
Arranged by Mona Rejino

Cheerfully (♩ = 116)

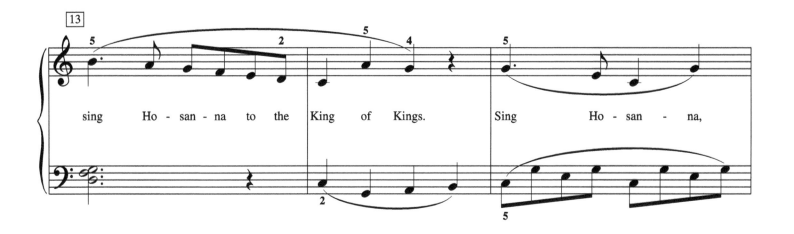

sing Ho - san - na to the King of Kings. Sing Ho - san - na,

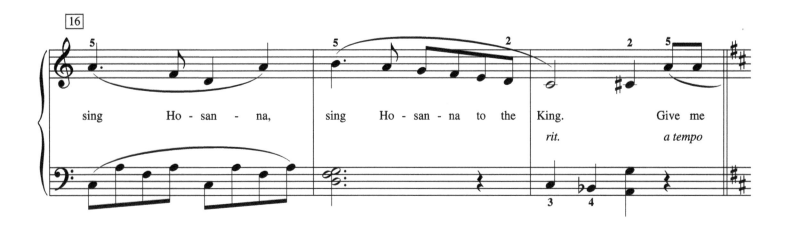

sing Ho - san - na, sing Ho - san - na to the King. Give me
rit. *a tempo*

oil in my lamp, keep me burn - ing. ___ Give me oil in my lamp, I

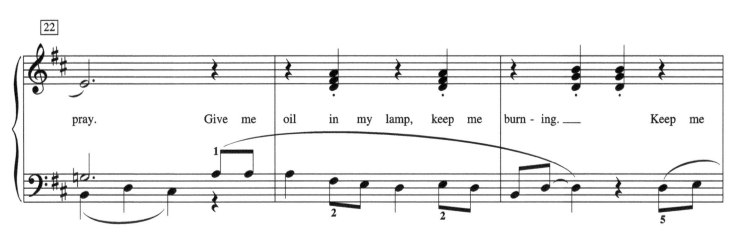

pray. Give me oil in my lamp, keep me burn - ing. ___ Keep me

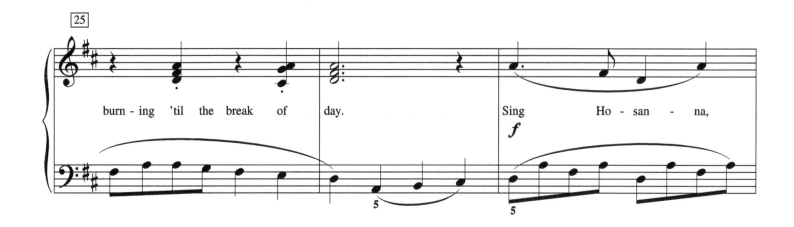

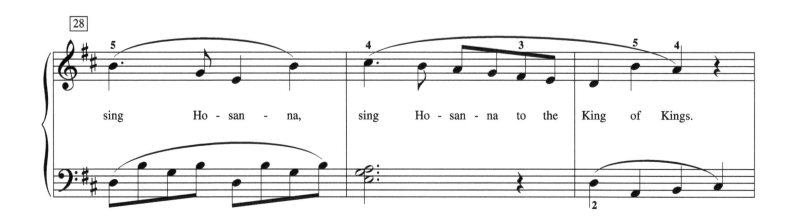

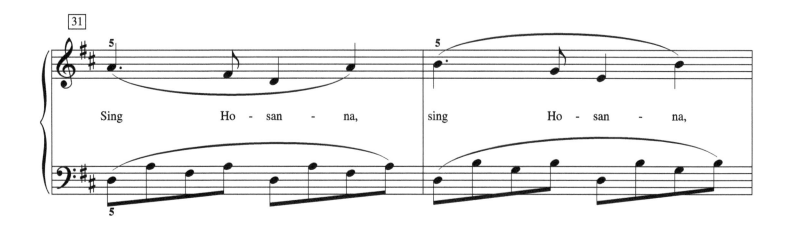

Let The Lower Lights Be Burning

Words and Music by
Philip P. Bliss
Arranged by Fred Kern

Hal Leonard Student Piano Library

The *Hal Leonard Student Piano Library has great music and solid pedagogy delivered in a truly creative and comprehensive method. It's that simple. A creative approach to learning using solid pedagogy and the best music produces skilled musicians! Great music means motivated students, inspired teachers and delighted parents. It's a method that encourages practice, progress, confidence, and best of all – success.*

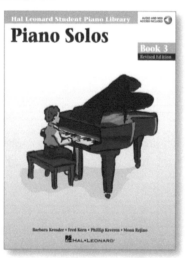

PIANO LESSONS BOOK 1
00296177 Book/Online Audio $9.99
00296001 Book Only $7.99

PIANO PRACTICE GAMES BOOK 1
00296002 .... $7.99

PIANO SOLOS BOOK 1
00296568 Book/Online Audio $9.99
00296003 Book Only $7.99

PIANO THEORY WORKBOOK BOOK 1
00296023 .... $7.50

PIANO TECHNIQUE BOOK 1
00296563 Book/Online Audio $8.99
00296105 Book Only $7.99

NOTESPELLER FOR PIANO BOOK 1
00296088 .... $7.99

TEACHER'S GUIDE BOOK 1
00296048 .... $7.99

PIANO LESSONS BOOK 2
00296178 Book/Online Audio $9.99
00296006 Book Only $7.99

PIANO PRACTICE GAMES BOOK 2
00296007 .... $8.99

PIANO SOLOS BOOK 2
00296569 Book/Online Audio $8.99
00296008 Book Only $7.99

PIANO THEORY WORKBOOK BOOK 2
00296024 .... $7.99

PIANO TECHNIQUE BOOK 2
00296564 Book/Online Audio $8.99
00296106 Book Only $7.99

NOTESPELLER FOR PIANO BOOK 2
00296089 .... $6.99

PIANO LESSONS BOOK 3
00296179 Book/Online Audio $9.99
00296011 Book Only $7.99

PIANO PRACTICE GAMES BOOK 3
00296012 .... $7.99

PIANO SOLOS BOOK 3
00296570 Book/Online Audio $8.99
00296013 Book Only $7.99

PIANO THEORY WORKBOOK BOOK 3
00296025 .... $7.99

PIANO TECHNIQUE BOOK 3
00296565 Book/Enhanced CD Pack $8.99
00296114 Book Only $7.99

NOTESPELLER FOR PIANO BOOK 3
00296167 .... $7.99

PIANO LESSONS BOOK 4
00296180 Book/Online Audio $9.99
00296026 Book Only $7.99

PIANO PRACTICE GAMES BOOK 4
00296027 .... $6.99

PIANO SOLOS BOOK 4
00296571 Book/Online Audio $8.99
00296028 Book Only $7.99

PIANO THEORY WORKBOOK BOOK 4
00296038 .... $7.99

PIANO TECHNIQUE BOOK 4
00296566 Book/Online Audio $8.99
00296115 Book Only $7.99

PIANO LESSONS BOOK 5
00296181 Book/Online Audio $9.99
00296041 Book Only $8.99

PIANO SOLOS BOOK 5
00296572 Book/Online Audio $9.99
00296043 Book Only $7.99

PIANO THEORY WORKBOOK BOOK 5
00296042 .... $8.99

PIANO TECHNIQUE BOOK 5
00296567 Book/Online Audio $8.99
00296116 Book Only $8.99

ALL-IN-ONE PIANO LESSONS
00296761 Book A – Book/Online Audio $10.99
00296776 Book B – Book/Online Audio $10.99
00296851 Book C – Book/Online Audio $10.99
00296852 Book D – Book/Online Audio $10.99

Prices, contents, and availability subject to change without notice.

www.halleonard.com

POPULAR SONGS
HAL LEONARD STUDENT PIANO LIBRARY

The **Hal Leonard Student Piano Library** has great songs, and you will find all your favorites here: Disney classics, Broadway and movie favorites, and today's top hits. These graded collections are skillfully and imaginatively arranged for students and pianists at every level, from elementary solos with teacher accompaniments to sophisticated piano solos for the advancing pianist.

Adele
arr. Mona Rejino
Correlates with HLSPL Level 5
00159590..............................$12.99

The Beatles
arr. Eugénie Rocherolle
Correlates with HLSPL Level 5
00296649.............................. $12.99

Irving Berlin Piano Duos
arr. Don Heitler and Jim Lyke
Correlates with HLSPL Level 5
00296838..............................$14.99

Broadway Favorites
arr. Phillip Keveren
Correlates with HLSPL Level 4
00279192..............................$12.99

Chart Hits
arr. Mona Rejino
Correlates with HLSPL Level 5
00296710..............................$8.99

Christmas at the Piano
arr. Lynda Lybeck-Robinson
Correlates with HLSPL Level 4
00298194..............................$12.99

Christmas Cheer
arr. Phillip Keveren
Correlates with HLSPL Level 4
00296616..............................$8.99

Classic Christmas Favorites
arr. Jennifer & Mike Watts
Correlates with HLSPL Level 5
00129582..............................$9.99

Christmas Time Is Here
arr. Eugénie Rocherolle
Correlates with HLSPL Level 5
00296614..............................$8.99

Classic Joplin Rags
arr. Fred Kern
Correlates with HLSPL Level 5
00296743..............................$9.99

Classical Pop – Lady Gaga Fugue & Other Pop Hits
arr. Giovanni Dettori
Correlates with HLSPL Level 5
00296921..............................$12.99

Contemporary Movie Hits
arr. by Carol Klose, Jennifer Linn and Wendy Stevens
Correlates with HLSPL Level 5
00296780..............................$8.99

Contemporary Pop Hits
arr. Wendy Stevens
Correlates with HLSPL Level 3
00296836..............................$8.99

Cool Pop
arr. Mona Rejino
Correlates with HLSPL Level 5
00360103..............................$12.99

Country Favorites
arr. Mona Rejino
Correlates with HLSPL Level 5
00296861..............................$9.99

Disney Favorites
arr. Phillip Keveren
Correlates with HLSPL Levels 3/4
00296647..............................$10.99

Disney Film Favorites
arr. Mona Rejino
Correlates with HLSPL Level 5
00296809 ....$10.99

Disney Piano Duets
arr. Jennifer & Mike Watts
Correlates with HLSPL Level 5
00113759..............................$13.99

Double Agent! Piano Duets
arr. Jeremy Siskind
Correlates with HLSPL Level 5
00121595..............................$12.99

Easy Christmas Duets
arr. Mona Rejino & Phillip Keveren
Correlates with HLSPL Levels 3/4
00237139..............................$9.99

Easy Disney Duets
arr. Jennifer and Mike Watts
Correlates with HLSPL Level 4
00243727..............................$12.99

Four Hands on Broadway
arr. Fred Kern
Correlates with HLSPL Level 5
00146177..............................$12.99

Frozen Piano Duets
arr. Mona Rejino
Correlates with HLSPL Levels 3/4
00144294..............................$12.99

Hip-Hop for Piano Solo
arr. Logan Evan Thomas
Correlates with HLSPL Level 5
00360950..............................$12.99

Jazz Hits for Piano Duet
arr. Jeremy Siskind
Correlates with HLSPL Level 5
00143248..............................$12.99

Elton John
arr. Carol Klose
Correlates with HLSPL Level 5
00296721..............................$10.99

Joplin Ragtime Duets
arr. Fred Kern
Correlates with HLSPL Level 5
00296771..............................$8.99

Movie Blockbusters
arr. Mona Rejino
Correlates with HLSPL Level 5
00232850..............................$10.99

The Nutcracker Suite
arr. Lynda Lybeck-Robinson
Correlates with HLSPL Levels 3/4
00147906..............................$8.99

Pop Hits for Piano Duet
arr. Jeremy Siskind
Correlates with HLSPL Level 5
00224734..............................$12.99

Sing to the King
arr. Phillip Keveren
Correlates with HLSPL Level 5
00296808..............................$8.99

Smash Hits
arr. Mona Rejino
Correlates with HLSPL Level 5
00284841..............................$10.99

Spooky Halloween Tunes
arr. Fred Kern
Correlates with HLSPL Levels 3/4
00121550..............................$9.99

Today's Hits
arr. Mona Rejino
Correlates with HLSPL Level 5
00296646..............................$9.99

Top Hits
arr. Jennifer and Mike Watts
Correlates with HLSPL Level 5
00296894..............................$10.99

Top Piano Ballads
arr. Jennifer Watts
Correlates with HLSPL Level 5
00197926..............................$10.99

Video Game Hits
arr. Mona Rejino
Correlates with HLSPL Level 4
00300310..............................$12.99

You Raise Me Up
arr. Deborah Brady
Correlates with HLSPL Level 2/3
00296576..............................$7.95

7777 W. BLUEMOUND RD. P.O. BOX 13819 MILWAUKEE, WI 53213

Visit our website at **www.halleonard.com**